I Can See a Sheep!

by Cameron Macintosh

OXFORD
UNIVERSITY PRESS
AUSTRALIA & NEW ZEALAND

I can see a sheep.

The sheep is in the shed.

I can see a hen.

4

The hen is high up on a rail.

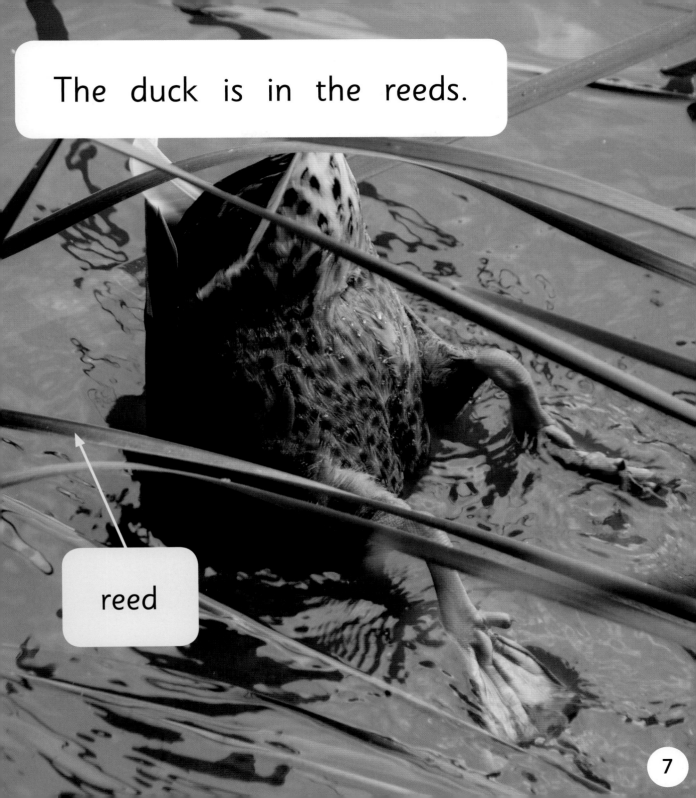

The duck is in the reeds.

reed

The goat is in the pen.

I can see
a foal.

The foal is in the sun.

I can see a rabbit.

The rabbit is in the run at night.

The dog runs along the road.